FOOTNOTES

David J. Forsyth

Rock's Mills Press
Oakville, Ontario
2020

Published by
Rock's Mills Press
www.rocksmillspress.com

Copyright © 2020 by David J. Forsyth
Introduction copyright © 2020 by Alan Bishop
All rights reserved. Published by arrangement with the author.

No part of this book may be used, reproduced, stored in or introduced into a retrieval system, or transmitted in any form or by any means (electronic, mechanical, photocopying, recording or otherwise) without the prior consent in writing of the publisher.

Contents

TITLE	PAGE
Ever Green	1
A Life Nonetheless	2
Portrait of Thought	3
Cycle of Love	4
Death	5
Vagrant Wind	6
Firefight	7
The Nam	8
To Michael	9
Walking Point	10
Your Turn	11
Love	12
Midsummer Miracle	13
I Never Bought My Dad a Drink	14
Relativity	15
The Horse and Groom	16
Cold War Retrospect	18
Together	19
White-Haired Warrior	20
Day's End	22
Seasons Past	24
The Beacon	25
Sermon of The Harp	26
The Pall Bearer	27
Tribute	28
London Boy	29
Atlantic City	31
If I Was God	32
Crumbs on a Yellow Plate	33
Hug Your Papa	34
Last Friday	35
Accumulated Tears	36
While I'm Asleep	37
Christmas Morning	39
The Pain, The Joy and Love Amassed	40
1962	42
The Breaker	43
Snowflake Whimsy	44
The Terrorist	45
The Witch of Winter	46
Devonshire Water	47
Vision	48
A Time to Cry	49
Candle Light	50
Enduring Love	51

Ghosts of Christmas Past	52
In The Shadow of Death	53
Memories of Trisha	54
Tic-Tic-Tock	55
Remembering Alice	56
Jack's Last Day	57

Foreword

David Forsyth's collection of more than fifty lyrics written over sixty years (1959 to 2020) is a satisfying and inspiring gift to readers.

These are well-crafted, emotionally powerful poems, often morally challenging in theme and thought, but always accessible. Moreover, added to each poem is a recent authorial comment which extends the poem's relevance, and contributes to the evolution of a virtual autobiography.

There are memories from childhood ("Ten hot summers chasing toads,/Playing ball and skipping stones,/Seeking love down dusty roads ...") and the sad memory of lost connection with his now-deceased father ("I never bought my Dad a drink").

Several of the poems rejoice in loving relationships, especially with his wife and grandchildren—the latter resulting in what is perhaps the collection's most optimistic, humorous and memorable poem, "Hug Your Papa" ("Your head will fall off if you fail/To tighten all the screws;/Your toes will drop off if you don't/Keep them inside your shoes ..." Read it, find out how it ends!).

Many of the poems are deeply serious, concerned with troubling topical issues and events. Contemporary international conflict—the Vietnam War, Northern Ireland Troubles, the Cold War—all impose a painful awareness of suffering and loss ("For all the soldiers throughout time,/Empty places at the table,/Forgotten victims of a crime ...").

Death is the topic of many poems, notably the deaths of the poet's father and grandfathers. But these are not poems of lamentation, they are primarily poems of meditation, intense meditation. They are poems to read, poems to remember and re-read, poems that will connect with your own life and thought, poems to reconsider. They are deceptively simple, and always accessible. They matter.

Read them!

ALAN BISHOP, D.Phil.
Hamilton, Ontario
2020

Ever Green

The pine stands tall in autumn rest,
Majestic, proud and green.
The mountain ash, the elm, the oak,
Each withered, burnt, a tired has-been.

Their beauty shed, consumed by frost,
Now pines alone are seen.
All others bare, their leaves decayed,
The lofty pine is ever green.

1959

I don't recall when I began writing poetry, nor when I fell in love with trees. Growing up on a farm likely contributed to both because time passed slowly in rural Ontario in the 1950s. I had time to ponder everything I encountered. Like most of my early poems, many of the trees with which I grew up are gone now. "Ever Green" is a survivor from my first year of secondary school when I was fifteen years old.

A Life Nonetheless

An ant, by crawling on the floor,
Disturbed a maiden dear to me.
I swiftly snuffed its frail life out
Though didn't, in the dim light see
What soon was to awaken me.

In early morning, after hours
Of comfort fine and peaceful sleep,
I saw a writhing figure, maimed,
Among the carpet fibers deep.
I pray the Lord his soul to keep.

My eyes endorsed the awful truth.
I gasped in horror at the thought
Of all the suffering and pain.
A meager life was all he sought,
And petty harm might he have wrought.

Most skillful hands in all the world
Could not repair the damage done,
And so I quickly sinned again
To end the pain inflicted one –
To stop the torture I'd begun.

I sat in dedicated thought
Of one whose life though short and small,
Meant just as much to that poor ant
As do the lives of *men* that fall.
That ant's demise I oft recall.

JUNE 1965

Much of my early poetry, including "A Life Nonetheless," was written for my own entertainment, whereas later works were born of passion and emotion. The event that inspired this work was actually a memory from several years earlier though obviously one that had given me pause for thought. I still murder spiders occasionally, but their deaths are due to an irrational fear, not the indifference I showed this poor creature.

Portrait of Thought

An artist paints not with a brush,
Nor writes a poet with a pen.
They each create with common tool;
The worthy deeds and thoughts of men.

I am a painter; poet not
And yet alone, we strive as one
To tell of feelings deep within;
A lonely struggle seldom won.

So in my comrade's stead I stand.
In his domain, I dare to paint
With words, not pigments to portray
My humble thoughts without restraint.

APRIL 1964 – OCTOBER 1965

I began my career as a commercial artist and viewed my poetry as outside of my skill set and a field in which I had no legitimacy. "A Portrait of Thought" is an acknowledgement of my appropriation of words in place of brush and canvas.

Cycle of Love

I know now why the summer winds
Blow lightly o'er the trees,
Why leaves of crimson, brown and gold
Dance on autumn's breeze.

Why crisp and cool, the winter chill
Slides darkly through bare limbs,
'Til greening buds of promise flirt
With warm, spring, southern winds.

JULY 1971

Reflecting on a number of long past romances, I wrote "Cycle of Love" as a metaphor for teenage relationships which, like seasons of the year, begin with great promise, grow weary over time and end in disappointment, but which by coming to an end make the next relationship possible.

Death

Nothing is distributed
More evenly than death.
There is no way the balance
Can be tampered with.

The only thing we know for sure
Is death will follow birth.
Most precious of all treasures is
Our time upon this earth.

1971

Years after rendering first aid to a four-year old boy who'd been struck by a car, I was haunted by the question of whether or not he had survived. Somewhat shaken at the time, I had deliberately avoided knowing the outcome, and kept the incident to myself. I was seventeen and invincible before the encounter, but at that moment I came to understand the value of life. "Death" was written nine years later.

Vagrant Wind

Through dark of night and sunlit day,
Of powers barely known,
From deep within to haunt my way,
A vagrant wind has blown.

It seeps and creeps into my brain,
Devouring conscious thought,
Inspiring mists of peace and pain.
In vacant eyes it's caught.

It thunders through my mind's back door
To fall on formless ears
And deafen with a silent roar,
Inspiring smiles and tears.

Suspended in a timeless sea,
Alone, with others there,
The vagrant wind, a *memory*,
Blows from and to nowhere.

8 JULY 1975

"Vagrant Wind" is about memories, some happy and uplifting, others sad and uncomfortable. They seem to come from nowhere, interrupting our lives for no apparent reason. Then they evaporate into thin air with the promise of returning again at some random moment in the future.

Firefight

We fought together,
Each one
Alone.

1989

I never experienced combat, nor lived through a Canadian-declared war, but I did enjoy a part-time relationship with two military regiments, so I take a substantial interest in the military experiences of others. In spite of the camaraderie among combatants, each individual is in reality alone in his or her struggle to survive both physically and mentally.

The Nam

With misty thoughts of home and love,
Of memories interlaced,
A warrior – a little boy,
His innocence erased
By screams and pleas and sticky blood;
By leeches, rats and rain
While thudding, thumping walls of sound
Collide within his brain

On steaming, muddy jungle trails
Consumed with breathless fear,
When nothing else exists beyond
The self, the now, the here –
Alone, he crawls through Hell and slime
And prays he will survive.
His brothers leave without farewell,
Some butchered, yet alive.

All heirs to horror, guilt and hate,
They weep, and wince, and stare,
But only those who have smelled death
Can know the whole nightmare.
A veteran now at forty-one,
And still sometimes he cries.
Once, Satan crept inside his head
And lives yet in his eyes.

1989

Those who have never experienced war must wonder how they would react if their courage was tested on the battlefield. During the 1970s and 1980s I read numerous non-fiction accounts of the Viet Nam War in an effort to understand how young men cope with the terror of battle and the horror of killing. Those narratives inspired "The Nam" in honour of those who found the courage to fulfil the expectations of their country, their commanders and their comrades.

To Michael

Not because I know him well,
But because . . .
He's been to Hell.

1989

I had the honour of working with one of Canada's most decorated police officers, a veteran of the United States Marine Corps who served at Khe Sahn, Dong Ho, Hue City and Hoi An, Vietnam. Though I never knew him well, I admire his courage and his integrity.

Walking Point

Enveloped in a leafy sponge,
My stomach filled with terror,
The scent of gun oil on my hands,
Death's angel's name is *Error*.

1989

Inspired by a first-person account of jungle warfare, these four lines were written in response to a so-called "cherry" who made a careless mistake due to inexperience. The brevity of the poem is meant to be symbolic of the young man's short life.

Your Turn

Have you ever seen a worm from down below,
Or smelled lilac when bare branches catch the snow?
Do you think the clouds look back when you look up?
Could a daisy ever love a buttercup?

Have you lived so long that you now understand
Every detail of every mystery at hand?
Should you sit and wait till life is done with you,
Or jump in, and ask, and feel, and think and do?

Never waste a breath of wind nor drop of rain;
Don't forget to feel the sun and board that train.
It's your turn to have a life – are you afraid?
When it's gone, what use of time will you have made?

MARCH 1991

While every new experience contains an element of risk, the rewards are often worth stepping outside our comfort zone. "Your Turn" is an appeal to those who are afraid to fly or try an unfamiliar food; those who just can't bring themselves to take a chance; people who regularly retreat to the security of inaction. The poem is a light-hearted appeal to make better use of the time we have allotted to us.

Love

A flower grows that never dies,
The seed of which is caring.
Eternity may pass and still
Its worth eludes comparing.

It warms you through the morning frost
And quells the fear of midnight.
Its silent music soothes your pain
And bathes your soul in moonlight.

By invitation or without,
Through one's design or fortune,
Without apparent cause, it's born
And fills your life with someone.

2 AUGUST 1992

"Love" was written about midway through a marriage that has now endured for fifty-five years. By the time the poem was written, our children had all married and my wife and I were enjoying our freedom along with our first grandchild.

Mid-Summer Miracle

From the breath of her mother
And Daddy's warm love;
A faint whisper from Grandma's lips,
In the midst of the summer,
From heaven above,
Came an angel with pink finger-tips.

Like the feeling that dwells
In a warm sunny morn',
Her blue eyes and wee smile evoke
Special happiness, shared
When a parent's first-born
Adds one more to our loved little folk.

There's a softness that touches
Old hearts only once.
Then mortality ceases to be.
In a sweet cherub face
That evolved o'er nine months,
There's a glow only Grandpa can see.

28 JULY 1992

"Mid-Summer Miracle" is an attempt to capture the magic of seeing one's grandchild for the first time.

I Never Bought My Dad a Drink

Sometimes,
The mirror looks at me.
I think my Dad stands there.
Again I look. It's me,
So was *he* ever here?

Sometimes,
I hear my voice and think,
"My Dad said that," and yet
It's gone as quick as wink.
I wonder about that.

Whiskey–
Rye whiskey's what he drank,
With ginger over ice.
Then quietly, he sank.
I watched through naive eyes.

Whiskey–
'Been gone four years this fall;
Sometimes I sit and think,
What nags me most of all?
I never bought my Dad a drink.

1994

My late father had a drinking problem, though neither he nor any member of the family ever uttered the word 'alcoholic' in relation to his addiction. It never interfered with his employment, and though he often drank to excess, he didn't exhibit the behaviours normally attributed to a drunk.

After his death, I regretted my silence on the matter. It wasn't that I felt a need to confront his compulsion to drink. In fact, I wished I had given him some indication that his affliction didn't in any way detract from my love and respect for him. Perhaps he would have understood if, just once, I had bought him a drink.

Relativity

Time, a constant cannot be,
When perceived by you and me
Since *your* short life is just begun
While my own time is almost done.

1994

At forty-nine years of age, I was struck by how quickly the years were passing and thought about my grandchildren, then one and three years old. To children, a year seems a very long time, and while I acknowledge the futility of the challenge, I wish I could convey to them the value of time.

The Horse and Groom

'Twas a Conlon bomb in Guildford;
A Conlon bomb indeed.
'Twas a Conlon bomb for fifteen years
Before the four were freed.

'Twas a Belfast boy in Bailey
And a Belfast father too.
'Twas a Belfast boy who loved his Da,
Every word they spoke was true.

'Twas an awful crime committed
By an evil gang of men.
'Twas a hopeless cause defended there,
In the shadow of Big Ben.

'Twas a deaf ear on the bench and
A vengeance in the air.
'Twas a deaf and a hate-blind jury;
Truth lost in its cold, hard stare.

'Twas a trial of lies and lying
After threats and beatings too.
'Twas a trial without a conscience, and
The suppression of a clue.

'Twas a time of pain and suffering
For the families – victims all.
'Twas a time of tears and of grieving
And a cold, high, grey stone wall.

'Twas a God-damned shame for Britain;
Gerry and Guiseppe too.
'Twas a God-damned shame for Scotland Yard,
When the awful thing was through.

'Twas a sickly Patty dying;
Being Cath'lic was his crime.

'Twas a sickly daddy died alone,
While his son was serving time.

'Twas a mother's love eternal,
And a wife's love for her man.
'Twas a mother's faint hope for justice,
Betrayed by a legal plan.

'Twas a long, hard time they suffered;
Five thousand grey days and more.
'Twas a long, hard sentence served within,
For stealing cash from a whore.

'Twas a man's life gone forever,
And a boy's life wasted too.
'Twas a woman's life and her children's;
An injustice done to you.

'Tis a story of a young man,
And a tale that should be told.
'Tis a story we must tell until
Every man's son has grown old.

1 SEPTEMBER 1994

During Northern Ireland's "troubles," I felt only contempt for The IRA's behaviour, but when several members of a Belfast family were wrongly convicted of bombing two Guildford pubs in the name of the IRA, my sense of justice outweighed any bias I may have harboured toward Northern Ireland's Catholics.

Gerry Conlon only came to the attention of police because he stole £700 from a prostitute in 1974. Still, he and his father, Giuseppe, were subsequently charged with crimes related to the Guildford pub bombings, and were convicted on the basis of fabricated evidence and confessions extracted through torture and threats. After serving almost fifteen years, the men were exonerated, and Gerry was released, but by then, his father had died of illness in prison.

Following his release from prison, Gerry Conlon authored a book titled "Proved Innocent." Then, in 1993, the Conlon story was reiterated in a movie titled "In The Name of the Father." Moved by the injustice of their conviction and suffering as depicted in the movie, I wrote "The Horse and Groom."

Cold War Retrospect

A fleet of icy missiles
Pursue predestined arcs
Within the neurons of our fear.
T'would render flesh to quarks.

Revulsion dwells within the skull;
A chill ascends the spine
As rockets trace precision routes
Through shadows of the mind.

1995

As a child, I lived through a tense geopolitical period known as the Cold War. While it officially lasted from 1947 to 1991, it became most noticeable to me in the late 1950s when news reports turned their attention to American missile silos and family fall-out shelters. Though the threat of nuclear conflict loomed, I didn't give it much thought as a child, but I learned long afterward that 60 percent of American children suffered from nightmares about nuclear attacks. I find it ironic that the Cold War's only victims were harmed by the publicity surrounding the West's defense systems rather than by the enemy's missiles.

Together

Throughout our life, I walk with you
O'er green resilient path or glaring sand,
And when your time on earth is through,
I'll be there still to hold your hand.

22 OCTOBER 1995

"Together" is a self-evident promise to a loved one that she will be loved, even after she has passed.

White-Haired Warrior

It's said that, freedom is not free.
There is a mandatory fee.
The cost is more than you might think,
And *you* can never pay the bill
Because the debt's been paid by me.

I'm the pilot; down and missing
On behalf of unborn offspring.
I'm the sailor lost at sea
And the prisoner who survived
Hunger, fear, lice and tapping.

I have memories of pain,
Warm blood and fever; rats and rain.
You have forgotten – I don't care.
I only wish I *could* forget.
Perhaps if I could go insane …

I'm comforted by alcohol.
My name appears *not* on The Wall.
I have wheels where you have legs,
And still, I flinch when thunder claps
And linger well beyond last call.

White-haired warrior on the ward,
Rocking slowly back and forward,
Staring blankly at the wall
Of a mental institution;
Seen by others as a coward.

My body twitches when I sleep.
The scars are ugly, and they're deep.
I'm the wounded, screaming "Medic!"
I'm the body in the bag;
On my toe, a fucking tag.

1995

In 1995, my thick, dark hair of the 1960s was gone, and it occurred to me that white-haired veterans of the Vietnam War were still living with the memories and pain of their experience, while I had conveniently filed my memories of the period away in some quiet corner of my mind. I wrote "White-haired Warrior" as a form of penance for forgetting.

Day's End

Now, late in the evening,
In darkness,
Recalling events of the day.
Alone with my thoughts
Of earlier sharing.
I feel
A sadness for lost opportunity,
Regrets
And fantasies of things that might have been,
And yet,
Happy to have had
A role.
I sigh.

Who am I,
Who was I, and
Who will I be?
I cry.

I miss her.
I miss me.
I miss us, and
Then *I* die.

7 MARCH 1997

Often, the works of poets are repeatedly interpreted by critics and scholars until consensus determines their meaning though I wonder how close they've actually come to the author's intent. Sometimes, long after my poems have been written, I worry that their meaning might be so obscure that my ideas will not survive. "Day's End" is one such example.

   I wrote the work after contemplating what I might feel if my wife predeceased me. As metaphors like "late in the evening" are somewhat enigmatic, I've supplemented the poem with a line-by-line interpretation as a one-time experiment. While decidedly unconventional, I believe this eccentricity might be appreciated by some readers.

Now, late in the evening,
nearing the end of my life

In darkness,
following the loss of my wife

Recalling events of the day.
remembering our life together

Alone with my thoughts
unable to share them with her

Of earlier sharing.
our life together

I feel
mourning her loss

A sadness for lost opportunity,
did she know how I loved her?

Regrets
for the things I might have said or done

And fantasies of things that might have been,
unattained shared goals

And yet,
still

Happy to have had
I am grateful

A role.
to have lived

I sigh.
acceptance of the way things are

Who am I,
what inherent value have I?

Who was I, and
did I have an impact on the world?

Who will I be?
will I be remembered, and if so, how?

I cry.
sad that my love has left me, and that my end is near

I miss her.
my deceased wife

I miss me.
the person I was when we were together

I miss us, and
the "us" that neither of us could have been individually

Then *I* die.
the last remnant of "us" (our life together) is gone

Seasons Past

Ten warm springs just slipped away,
Blurry memories, soft and warm,
Savoured on that windy day
When my family sang to me.
I didn't know that I was free.

Ten hot summers chasing toads,
Playing ball and skipping stones;
Seeking love down dusty roads
In simmering, shimmering August highs,
Idealism in my eyes.

Ten cool autumns, then induction,
Humping ammo through the jungle,
Hating leeches with a passion,
Watching luckless comrades fall;
Names now etched upon The Wall.

Ten frosty winter seasons gone,
Since our discharge papers freed us,
From horrors witnessed at Khe Sahn.
Seems like we were there forever
Might I forget? Hell, never!

1997

Seasons Past contrasts decades of childhood innocence and teenage idealism with those of adult responsibility and mid-life baggage, as a veteran of war might perceive them. To emphasize the contrast, the meter of the first stanza is reversed in the last stanza (7,7,7,7,8 vs. 8,8,8,8,7) and that of the second verse is reversed in the third (7,7,7,8,8 vs. 8,8,8,7,7).

The Beacon

To seek adventure on the sea,
I now embark; escape your light.
Keep safe. Embrace your love of me,
And keep it lit throughout the night.
Its loom I'll seek on my return,
So hold it high and shining bright.
Its flame within my heart will burn
Till in my arms I hold you tight.

20 DECEMBER 1998

"The Beacon" is a metaphor for a mariner's sweetheart. As the mariner embarks on a lengthy passage, he promises to return and pledges to be true to her.

Sermon of The Harp

I cried for a man; nay,
I cried for all mankind.
The Catholics, the Protestants,
All those whom sorrows find.

The earth is cool and damp,
The sod is green and yet,
'Neath saline drops of Godless pain
The grass, with blood, is wet.

Compelled to serve their God,
Engaged in endless sin,
Each hates the other, bombs and kills;
No chance have they to win.

When will they understand?
When will they end their shame?
A million of God's souls ascend
And all will bear the blame.

1999

Because I have both Roman Catholic and Protestant ancestry, I perceive Ireland's troubles from a somewhat neutral perspective and find myself conflicted though not as one might expect. While entirely opposed to this generation's violence, I understand that the perpetrators are themselves victims of intense religious indoctrination from a very early age. While I believe steadfastly in accountability for one's behaviour, I cannot ignore how one's 'free will' is degraded by intense parental and ecclesiastical brain-washing. Should each successive generation be held in greater contempt for their violence – or for passing their hatred on to their children?

The Pallbearer

Now lightly laden with crisp, yellow leaves,
A refuge for a tired and dying few,
The silver surface slides beneath the bridge.
Its refugees then disappear from view.

The unrelenting, Jack-driven passage
Of cold and slippery liquid drains away,
Its cargo borne swiftly toward the sea.
Each corpse the current promised to convey.

Then sudden recognition in the veins
Within a leaf below me scudding by.
Staring past my worn-out sneakered toes,
Searching for an explanation. Why?

Old watery eyes strain to see below,
A leaf whose every detail known to me
Floats by. A chill invades my soul, and then
With sudden comprehension – *I am free*!

1999

Imagine standing on a bridge in autumn, looking down, and watching fallen leaves being swept out of view beneath the bridge. Each unique leaf represents a life, and every life comes to an end. In a flash of inspiration, you imagine an approaching leaf is your life, and its disappearance beneath the bridge is not far in the future. At first, the thought is frightening, but then, you realize that knowing your time is limited is, in itself, a gift.

Tribute

We hurried through the classroom door
And trod the road to Hell,
Sweet smelling bright-eyed girls behind;
Ahead, death's obscene smell.

Laughter and grins; then tears enough
To scrub them from our past
As we walked through the gates of Hell,
Our M-16s held fast.

We entered Satan's slaughterhouse
Proud-marching with the dead.
We helped them die. They helped us live.
They linger in my head.

Now, standing here before *The Wall*,
Recalling jungle rain,
The blood, the screams, the wide-eyed fear;
This tribute to their pain
Drips salty from my weathered cheek.
That's all I have to give
Beyond these words, inadequate,
From those of us who live.

1999

Survivor syndrome is a psychological condition that occurs when a person experiences feelings of guilt in response to surviving a traumatic event while others did not. As a Canadian, I wasn't expected to participate in the Vietnam War. Still, my exposure to daily television news coverage fostered empathy for young men in that war, many of whom went straight from school to military service. I witnessed their fear and pain almost within my reach as I sat comfortably on the sofa. I became obsessed with understanding the combatant's experience, and read every first-person account of the war I could find. I viewed a half-scale travelling replica of the Vietnam War Memorial when it came to Canada in the 1990s. While standing before The Wall, I was inspired to acknowledge the suffering and loss it represented. Later that day, I scribbled the first draft of the poem onto a scrap of paper.

London Boy

Born just before the century,
Remembered in the next,
A London boy from Forest Gate,
At fifteen, sailed toward his fate;
The worthy subject of this text.

Alone aboard a British ship,
Sailed he beyond his fear.
The voyage wet and cold and grim –
The crossing truly tested him.
In nineteen-ten he settled here.

His family followed in his steps.
Established in this land,
Until Britannia needed him;
Another passage, cold and grim –
He stood erect among the damned.

The trenches promised shelter from
The raging, distant guns.
Then, gas descended from above
And gripped him in its yellow glove;
A burning gift from Berlin's sons.

Returned to Bristol to recoup
Confined two months abed,
Then, married a sweet London miss;
Returned across the waves to bliss,
His khaki friends at Vimy dead.

Four girls he fathered, then a son –
The infant passed away.
His bride, exiled from Mum and Dad,
Though homesick, tired, and deeply sad,
Stood by his side through every day.

The Great Depression he endured;
He served in World War Two.
A pioneer – survived two wars –
He opened countless leaden doors,
Stood tall, and boldly walked on through.

4 JANUARY 2000

"London Boy" was written to honour my maternal grandfather. He grew up in London, England, and at fifteen years of age, emigrated to Canada on his own. He served in the Canadian Expeditionary Force, survived severe burns from an enemy mustard gas attack in World War I, and returned to the front line after his recovery. He married a Londoner during the war, returning with her to Canada where they raised a family together. My grandfather remained fit and courageous, enlisting in the Veteran's Guard of Canada during the Second World War and later, while in his seventies, helping a police officer physically subdue a suspect he was trying to arrest. He died just prior to his ninety-first birthday, a few hours after playing frisbee with two of his teen-aged great-grandchildren.

Atlantic City

O'er deck blew a chill, salty wind off the coast.
I emerged from my berth in mid-afternoon;
On watch with the skipper, I'd been until four,
And then, once again, through the morning 'til noon.

Forsaking the warmth of the cabin below,
I stood on our island of glass, peering west.
The Volvo thrummed low in some distant alcove;
My ears heard the drone – not my consciousness.

Five miles off our beam, inched the coast to the south,
The City, still north in a future to come,
Crouched on the horizon before the port bow.
Then dinner, coffee and a mug of dark rum.

The infamous town slid silently near,
Her landscape a bar graph; the sun edging low,
The pinks and the mauves of the evening merge
With darkness beyond the red neon's warm glow.

Awakened and brilliant, she ruled o'er the night,
Adorned in the language of voltage and amp.
I watched her, seduced by her scarlet embrace,
In evening-wear dressed, though she be a tramp.

Relieved at the end of that memorable watch,
The hour and The City slid into my past.
Bewitched by a dome of pink haze in the night,
I stood on the coach-roof and leaned on the mast.

4 JANUARY 2002

In the year 2001, while sailing northward off the east coast of the United States, I saw Atlantic City, New Jersey from a unique perspective. The occasion was particularly memorable because I viewed the metropolis against the sunset just as its commercial lighting began dominating the darkening sky. While reading my journal in the winter of 2001–2002, I felt compelled to record the scene in a poem. A prose description of the event can be found in "Too Cold for Mermaids," published in 2017.

If I Was God

If I was God,
I would *not* let children die.
Never again
Would parents cry out, 'Why?'
Had I the power,
I'd back the hands an hour
And let the children live
Until their parents die.

23 DECEMBER 2005

Already frustrated with the suffering and deaths of innocent children, I witnessed a very close friend cope with his daughter's terminal illness. About five weeks after I wrote "If I Was God," my friend's daughter died. He barely endured her loss and cried almost every day, until his pain ended with his own death twelve years later.

Crumbs on a Yellow Plate

Assembled awkwardly in groups,
Our voices hushed,
Warm gentle words of comfort spoke.
Her father – *crushed*.

The graveside tears behind us now,
We chat and chew
A lunch and softly speak of all
The years that flew.

A yellow plate and plastic fork,
In trash-bag tossed,
Tell nothing of the past nor her
Brief life, now lost.

Instead a few sweet crumbs upon
The plate remain,
Remnants of what no longer is.
We share the pain.

Her sunny day comes to an end.
Still un-consoled,
We hug, don coats, then turn and walk
Into the cold.

30 JANUARY 2007

On the anniversary of the death of a friend, I recalled the reception that followed her graveside service. As is customary, I drank a cup of coffee while chatting with family members and friends, and I ate a piece of cake served on a yellow paper plate. When the mourners began leaving the hall, I discarded the crumb littered plate, dropping it into a waste container along with a plastic fork. At that moment, I thought how tragic it was that, once the reception ended and everyone was gone, the only physical evidence that remained was a few cake crumbs on a yellow plate.

Hug Your Papa

Your head will fall off if you fail
To tighten all the screws;
Your toes will drop off if you don't
Keep them inside your shoes;

Your teeth will dribble down your chin,
Your lips will melt and drip,
Your big brown eyes just won't stay in,
Your vertebrae will slip;

Your brain will melt and ooze out of
Both ears, in gooey lumps,
Your knees will seize, your hair will fall
In tangled, hairy clumps.

If you don't hug your Papa now
And then, from time to time,
This curse will come and get you – No,
It's just a goofy rhyme!

10 NOVEMBER 2008

When our eight-year-old grandson visited, he liked to listen to me read Shel Silverstein poems, and I enjoyed his enthusiastic "hello" and "goodbye" hugs. One day, in anticipation of his next visit, I wrote "Hug Your Papa," and as I expected, he was delighted to hear me read it on several occasions thereafter.

Last Friday

Daddy died last Friday.
He was not Daddy, anymore.
Daddy died a bit each day
Four decades or more before.
I didn't cry.

And then he was my Dad.
Dad died some more, some time ago.
A weary aging man remained.
Yes, Dad died; his death was slow.
I didn't cry.

An old man died last week,
Released from loneliness and pain,
And for a fleeting moment
He was my Daddy again.
I cried.

17 MAY 2011

Relationships change over the years. In the beginning my father was my "Daddy," but as a married adult with children of my own, I and my "Dad" had a much more mature connection. In 1980 he moved to a small town in Northern Ontario to spend his retirement fishing and hunting. Separated thereafter by an eight- to nine-hour drive, we saw one another only once or twice a year for a decade.

That changed our relationship, his health declined, and his appearance changed too. I almost forgot who he really was until he died. Then I realized he had never stopped being the "Daddy" of my childhood.

"Last Friday" asserts that evolving connections between people never erase who we were at the beginning of the relationship.

Accumulated Tears

In young men strength runs deeper;
Just twelve when first I met the reaper.
September four of fifty-seven
My granddad packed his bags for heaven.
I didn't cry but understood
That he was gone; one day I would.

A boy named *Pumpkin* on the road –
And through my fingers his blood flowed,
I had no tears though later shook;
Another page turned in my book.
Death stopped by in sixty-three;
The Dallas book depository.

Then, tears so long behind a dam,
Began to drip in Viet Nam
Where fifty thousand Yank boys died.
I cried and cried though deep inside.
When Gran and Grandpa said goodbye
I knew, and still I whispered, "Why?"

They say time heals, but *they* don't know
How tears accumulate below
The surface, in a place unseen.
Each one is warm, wet, saline.
Now that I'm old, to quench my pain,
My tears cascade like monsoon rain.

12 JANUARY 2012

I wrote "Accumulated Tears" at the age of sixty-seven, when I noticed that controlling my emotions was becoming progressively more difficult. Others of similar age admitted to experiencing the same phenomenon, and it occurred to me that repeated exposure to the pain and suffering of others may have a long-term impact on our ability to cope with tragedy.

While I'm Asleep

Grieve little at my grave my dear,
For I was but a meagre speck.
If tears be in your eyes, then weep
On my behalf for each train wreck,
For all the wars in all the world,
For all the soldiers throughout time,
Empty places at the table,
Forgotten victims of a crime,
For ships that sank; for crews that drowned
And all the upturned trucks and cars,
For every child who won't grow up
And all those burned, and all their scars,
For every widow everywhere,
For all the drive-bys, drugs and pain
And every flight that crashed and burned,
For everyone who went insane,
Those imprisoned for their beliefs,
For every child lost in the woods,
Slaves and orphans, and refugees,
Typhoons, tornadoes, deadly floods
And rare diseases oversees,
And men who die for what is right,
Forgotten grans in nursing homes,
The hunkered homeless in the night,
The bombs of terrorists – the maimed
Those tortured on medieval racks,
Starvation and the holocaust,
And broken bodies on the tracks,
Avalanches and tsunamis
And homicide and suicide
And accidents involving guns
And moms and dads who wailed and cried.

I could continue endlessly.
More tragedy than I can tell,
Still all the tears that I could cry
Would be too few to cleanse this Hell!

Grieve little at my grave, I beg.
If tears be in your eyes, then weep
For all who suffer agony,
On my behalf *while I'm asleep.*

12 JANUARY 2012

Life has been good to me. I haven't suffered any significant hardships or faced any insurmountable setbacks. My inevitable end will be painful for those who love me, but the death of an old man is not tragic. "While I'm Asleep" is a reminder that tragedy is everywhere in this world, and those of us who escape unscathed should appreciate our good fortune and feel compassion for those who suffer.

Christmas Morning

What is it?
Is it mine?
I'm sure that it's something expensive and fine.
Don't shake it,
You'll break it.
Bright ribbons and wrappings and gold-coloured twine.

I found it
This morning,
Right under the tree with the rest of the gifts.
Let's see it,
Just give it!
There's frost on the window, chill air and snow drifts.

From the tree
To my hand . . .
Eyes wide with excitement, my gaze on it locks.
I grab it
(Politely);
I tear off the wrapping and stare at the box.

Fantastic!
I love it!
"Hold on; there's a problem," someone alluded.
What is it?
It can't be;
It says the batteries are not included.

10 DECEMBER 2015

Once a month, a dozen or more local authors and literary enthusiasts gather in Cayuga, Ontario to read and discuss the works of authors past and present. Occasionally, those of us who write share our own work with the group. Our December meeting invariably concerns works related to Christmas, and one year, I decided to write something especially for that gathering. "Christmas Morning" is a light-hearted celebration of new technology, but from the perspective of the late 1960s, when many toys became battery-operated.

The Pain, The Joy and Love Amassed

Leave no day, hour nor moment of your past
Behind; embrace the heat of yore again;
Recall the pain, the joy and love amassed.

Look to the shadows, in memory fast;
Feel the burn of loss. Touch the glow of win.
Leave no day, hour nor moment of your past

Behind, and keep the fire of life steadfast.
Fan the flames of recollection within;
Recall the pain, the joy and love amassed.

Welcome glimpses; grip them until at last,
Recollections grow to thickness from thin.
Leave no day, hour nor moment of your past

Behind; blow on the embers of long-past,
Ignite a blaze of places and of kin.
Recall the pain, the joy and love amassed.

Those memories upon the ash heap cast,
Rob heirs of witness, scrape flesh from skin.
Leave no day, hour nor moment of your past;
Recall the pain, the joy and love amassed.

18 JANUARY 2015

This poem was inspired by Dylan Thomas's "Do Not Go Gently Into That Good Night" which was read at the September 2014 Third-Thursday event in Cayuga, Ontario. It was my first exposure to the poetic form known as a villanelle. Subsequently, I challenged myself to create one of my own. My villanelle addresses the value of memory, imploring the reader to savour every experience of his or her life through recollection. I believe the stories of ordinary people are worth recording for future generations, and in the poem I refer to lost stories as being cast upon an ash heap.

The poem is a little tricky to read because there is a peculiar aspect to three of the poem's lines. Note that the first line remains incomplete until the initial word of the second line is read. i.e. "Leave no day, hour nor moment of your past" The word "behind," which appears at the start of the second line, completes the thought.

Since one requirement of a villanelle is that the initial line is repeated in the second, fourth and final stanzas, the anomaly is also repeated three times, though in the penultimate line, it could not be completed by the final line, since the rules call for that line to be the same as the poem's third line. That missing word, "behind," is symbolic of a lost memory.

1962

Downstairs Club
1962
black on black
thick, blue tobacco smoke
pulsing guitar
white-hot spotlight
John Lee Hooker
trickling beads of sweat
blues
Boom, Boom, Boom, Boom

20 JANUARY 2016

Inexplicably, every human culture has an ancient connection with music. What draws the human species to rhythmic beats and melodies? Most of us have persistent memories of at least one or two musical events. The one forever burned into my psyche is depicted in the poem "1962."

The Breaker

Eternal am I,
Now driven before the kraken's breath
Onto the essence of the hour-glass,
To spill De Beers-like to my death.
My last words thunder dark and bright
In deepest blue and foaming white.

Compelled to race on
'Neath the spell of the orbiting sphere,
I lick the land with a salty tongue.
Dragged from another place to here,
To my destiny am I true.
Sea birds peck at my residue.

My soul slips away;
My corpse lies not where I came to die,
A fish-like odour lingers there.
My life is spent; No one will cry.
A glorious end devoid of pain;
My brief headstone a mere, dark stain.

13 JANUARY 2016

In recent years, my wife and I have escaped a number of frigid Februarys by spending those months in Miramar Beach, Florida. I was thinking about that beach when I went to bed one night in January, and I began composing this poem in my head. Over the next two or three hours, I rose five times, crept into my den in the dark to sit at my computer and add a few more lines which might otherwise have been forgotten by morning.

The poem personifies the death of a wave as it crashes onto a beach and perhaps adds some perspective to human life and death. Human lives are, after all, as numerous as the waves absorbed by the sand and as certain to end with little or no lasting impact on the universe.

Snowflake Whimsy

One mid-winter mid-day a snowflake fell
Onto an eastbound ocean swell.
For weeks thereafter, consumed by laughter,
It rose and fell, and rose and fell.

18 DECEMBER 2017

Generally speaking, we, as individuals, have little impact on the big picture, but that doesn't mean that each tiny contribution doesn't matter.

The Terrorist

With hatred torn from sacred scripture,
In a split-second blast of instant death,
Bringing unspoken, exploding agony,
Leaving red-stained pavement under foot,
He seeks glory.

In a rain of red-hot, razor-edged steel,
A soup of torn flesh and shattered bone,
Limbless children, their futures stolen,
And victims painted with warm, red death,
He finds hell.

26 MARCH 2017

Terrorism is an evil beyond my comprehension. I simply can't imagine why someone would rather destroy than create. How does one decide that his God wants him to kill people he doesn't even know, children who will never know why they died? "The Terrorist" is nothing more than an expression of my anger. The metre is ragged and there are no rhyming lines because terrorism is ugly.

The Witch of Winter

Winter's boot tramps over pastures,
Wrapping fields in blue-white gauze,
Fetching sleep to once-green grasses,
And spreading ice on streams and ponds.

Liquid moonshine creeps o'er hillsides,
White-washing slopes with sacred light,
Bringing love to lads and lasses
With memories of a silver night.

Flickering flames of distant stars
Sparkle against black velvet sky.
Fingers tingle in spite of mittens;
The wisest owls refuse to fly.

Bleaching charm with cold indifference,
The light of dawn quick steals the night.
Then, silver chill turns warm and yellow;
The witch's dreamscape washed with light.

22 DECEMBER 2017

Standing quietly in a barnyard beneath a full moon on a crisp winter night is a rare experience these days. With most of the western world living in urban comfort and moving about inside heated vehicles, "The Witch of Winter" has become elusive. Sometimes, the price of exceptional beauty is discomfort. Find a quiet spot on a moonlit night, park the car, get out and just stand quietly looking about.

Devonshire Water

A carnival of froth descends
  'neath an ancient, time-torn bridge.
Down water-worn stone, it wetly slips
  like a scudding, grey cloud ridge
  o'er a windswept Devonshire moor.
The liquid white, raucous avalanche,
  on its endless, clambering race,
  dances among the ancient slates,
  descending at a stallion's pace,
  to seek refuge on the valley floor.

Alone, no witness to affirm
  its cool bubbling, boiling fall,
  it plunges toward a quiet pause,
  where pooled in a boggy sprawl
  on the ageless Devonshire moor,
  it sleeps at the feet of bumpy hills.
Anon the sun will draw it high
  and send it on its windy way
  to fall in droplets from the sky
  and dance once more to valley floor.

23 JANUARY 2018

The United Kingdom is the home of my ancestors as well as my favourite place in the world. I've been lucky to have been able to visit it many times, and I never tire of seeking out its villages and vistas. Recalling a past drive through Dartmoor National Park, I wrote "Devonshire Water" in an attempt to solidify a fading memory.

Vision

These eyes, once wide with youthful gaze,
Like Kodaks, sought souvenirs of life.
Amazing tools; they penetrate the haze,
A million images collected.

They have served their master faithfully.

What wisdom could within exist
Were life not acquired through such portals?
Seas sailed, peaks conquered, and young women kissed;
A billion images reflected,

Viewed and stored away within my brain.

Yet age shall wrought a body torn,
Plastic lenses enhance what is seen;
Encyclopaedic work since I was born.
A trillion images projected

Onto the canvas of memory.

ST. PATRICK'S DAY 2018

Aware that both my grandmother and my mother lost their sight towards the end of their lives, I sometimes reflect on the role that our eyes play in understanding our world though most of the time I don't give them much thought. "Vision" is a reminder to myself and others that sight is an incredible gift, one that should not to be taken for granted.

A Time to Cry

A farm-boy, barefoot and oft sun-burned,
Skinned knees and knuckles; wind-blown hair,
Shed ample tears to pain and childhood fear –
And when he didn't get his way.
But as he grew, the crying went away.

A grown man, too proud and somewhat brave,
From such behaviour doth refrain.
Naive is he; immune he thinks to pain.
Then came the war – The distant thud,
A nearby blast, the sticky, blood-soaked mud.

A sobbing mother, a wife, a lover,
A young girl's scream, "My daddy's dead!"
A stoic heart, once light, now turned to lead.
One glistening tear escapes his eye,
And trickles o'er his cheek. 'Tis time to cry.

18 JUNE 2019

Comfortably, with a mug of hot tea in my hand, I sat in the garden enjoying a fresh, warm, morning breeze. I was thinking about the book that I was writing, the most recently drafted chapters of which deal with war – not the Hollywood War; the war of military records, regimental diaries and yellowed photographs of real people. A tear formed in the corner of my eye, and I reached for my notebook and a pen.

Candlelight

I am but a flame, born of a spark long past;
Once bright and hot, and fuelled by molten wax.
With disregard, I burned the fuel of youth.
Shortly will I flicker before a heartless wind,
Weakly clinging to the fragile wick of life.
Near the end, I will shrink to a glowing ember;
One final gasp of smoke as I extinguish.
Where once I shone, there is naught but carbon,
And a memory of a once brilliant light.

14 JUNE 2019

"Candlelight" is a rather obvious metaphor for life and death because a candle flame's existence is similarly frail and finite. The poem reflects my conviction that we should shine brightly while we're able.

Enduring Love

I'll love you
'til every star
in the universe
grows cold.

19 DECEMBER 2019

I have decades-old memories of my wife telling our infant grandchildren, "I love you to the moon and back." Out of curiosity, I searched for the expression's origin, but the internet has become so corrupted with uninformed opinions and commercial interests that the quest appears hopeless. I wonder if anyone will ever research the origin of "I'll love you 'til every star in the universe grows cold."

Ghosts of Christmas Past

Lights on the Christmas tree abide,
Gifts, wrapped and bagged, beneath it hide.
In darkened upstairs room, a child
Sleeps in peace and mercy mild.

Lights bright without, yet dim within;
Cards sent to us from friends and kin
Bring good cheer to home and mantle.
In each window glows a candle.

Flames dance among the logs and fling
Sparks on the hearth while carols ring
Out softly in the chill night air
Beyond the wreathed front door somewhere.

Snow drifts adorn the window sill.
The night is crisp with frost, and still
A feast of turkey yet to come;
Tonight, a warming glass of rum.

Some oatmeal cookies on a plate
And glass of milk for him await
The morning, when excited eyes
Gaze upon toys and mitts and ties.

A warm contentment fills my heart.
This eve, though some live miles apart,
We embrace and laugh together.
It is the gift that I most treasure.

26 DECEMBER 2019

While I have many fond memories of my childhood, none can compare with the warm glow of past Christmases. I want to share that experience with others, and I wrote "Ghosts of Christmas Past" as my Christmas gift to all those who read it.

In The Shadow of Death

From the moment of our birth
We live in the shadow of death

>Some only hours or minutes
>Yet others bear witness
>To the passing of a century of change

Few comprehend their future
Or know when their end will come

>Whether victim of war or suicide
>Or quietly in our sleep
>We are each of us destined to die

From that very first breath, and so
We live in the shadow of death

20 DECEMBER 2019

We represent one of perhaps 10,000 generations of modern man (or woman as the case may be). Our lives are brief and death is inevitable. Understanding that reality is rather important if we are to contribute to the collective human experience in a meaningful way; if we are to awaken each day with a sense of purpose.

Memories of Trisha

Though I can't see you, I shall remember,
Though I can't touch you, you'll still be there,
I'll hear your words for many years yet,
And sense your presence everywhere.

Though you must leave the world I live in,
You've left your footprints in the snow.
You've shared your laughter, love, and tears,
And I'm so sad to see you go.

On quiet nights, I'm sure to miss you,
I'll want to call you on the phone,
Memories of you shall then sustain me,
When but for grief, I'm all alone.

18 NOVEMBER 2019

We tend to take our loved ones for granted until an accident or serious illness threatens to take them from us. Imagining what my life would be like without my spouse of more than fifty years, I wrote "Memories of Trisha."

Tic-Tic-Tock

So young, you do not see it passing
Yet I have watched it come – *and go.*
Your naive ears hear not the ticking;
The sweeping hand perceive you slow.

How fast the sweeping, tic-tic-ticking,
How quickly life doth come and go.
Your time draws nigh; your day for passing.
The hour is near when you will know.

Use wisely every crumb of living,
The weight is swinging to and fro.
The key is lost, the spring unwinding,
The day has come, and now – *you know.*

28 JUNE 2019

Time is indifferent to our needs and plods along whether or not we notice it passing. I wrote "Tic-Tic-Tock" because I feel it's important that we understand that from an early age. Waking up to find that our childhood is gone appears to be a universal experience, yet most of us don't get the hint. Then one day, we wake up and realize we're middle-aged! Still, some of us ignore the signs. Damned if we don't look in the mirror one morning at white hair and wrinkles, wondering how much time we have left to fulfil all those dreams we once had.

Remembering Alice

Alice came to visit in ninety-eight;
She brought along a loving heart, and strength.
A quiet child, she leaned into her fate.
For others, she would go to any length.

Eighteen, and filled with London sounds and smells,
She met a khaki promise from afar,
Then Alice saw her love endure the Hells
That test the courage of men in time of war.

Mustard gas, and shells, and fear, and worry,
Shared wordless in dark moments during leave.
An infant, then a marriage in a flurry;
By warp and weft of choices she did weave.

Scrawled postcards filled with love from Flanders flew.
Their love, their sunshine, could not stay the rain;
One day the last man died, and Alice knew
She'd never see her mum and dad again.

At sea aboard a troop-ship, westward bound,
The two endured each passing storm as one,
Called "Queen" by Mum and Dad, yet never crowned,
She raised four daughters; mourned a son.

Grandchildren filled her kitchen, lap and life;
Her values passed to each and every one.
A London child, a mother, and a wife;
In eighty-eight she passed, her story done.

5 MAY 2020

Alice left her London home and family in the summer of 1919 to begin a new life in Canada. She had married a Canadian soldier a year earlier, and sailed out of Liverpool aboard the S.S. Corsican along with her infant daughter. Already pregnant with her second child, she understood that she would almost certainly never see her parents again. Imagine, if you can, the anxiety and the fear that war-brides felt, and the courage it must have taken to endure that.

Jack's Last Day

He was a little man, but a ball of fire,
And I am surprised at the weight of his coffin.
Then I realize how many hopes and fears,
And how much courage and pain lie within.

Uneven ground amid tilted bronze markers
Staggers our steps to the distant, gaping, dark hole.
We six descendants, honoured to bear the weight
Of the casket, and the man, and his soul.

The Union Jack trumpets, "Here lies a hero"
A suitable title for the satin-wrapped man.
Through fixed eyes blurred by warm tears of remembrance,
I stare ahead at the gathered black clan.

The priest, in rich garments, The Book in his hands;
The widow, supported by family, shaken,
Await the most ghastly of rituals contrived
To inhume one so suddenly taken.

With putlogs bearing the weight of our burden,
We pallbearers re-join our wives standing alone.
A still moment passes, a bird chirps, and then
The low, mournful birth of a bagpipe's tone.

Tears streaming, hearts aching, we stand through the wail
Of the piper's lament, slow, lingering and sad.
The priest speaking words that all clergy recite.
Rigid, I stare at the piper's gay plaid.

Three decades have passed, and still the grief lingers,
His last day with us forever locked in my mind.
The sadness of losing his presence goes on,
A loss for his kin, a loss for mankind.

8 MAY 2020

John Albert Collier, 86th Machine Gun Battalion, Canadian Expeditionary Force, World War One, died in August of 1984, having lived ninety years, nine months and ten days. He was survived by his wife and 44 descendants, including the author of this poem.

About the Author

David J. Forsyth began life as a farm boy, running barefoot and shirtless through hay fields in summer and chasing frogs in a creek that ran through a neighbouring farm. He left school as a commercial artist, but spent most of his thirty-five-year pursuit of an income in supervisory and management roles in municipal government. His positions involved extensive copywriting, editing and technical writing, all of which helped to develop his writing skills. He describes himself as an amateur husband and father, genealogist, historian, mariner, explorer, and photographer.

"*I love water; sweet water (fresh) and blue water (salt). I like sailing on it, canoeing and kayaking over it, and photographing it; I also enjoy folk music, reading, British beers—I even have my own little pub called 'The Frog & Parrot'—and I'm always planning a trip somewhere. I've flown airplanes and drifted over southern Ontario in the basket of a hot-air balloon. I've canoed the French River, kayaked the Grand River, and sailed the Great Lakes and the eastern seaboard from Florida to Labrador. I've looked down on Scotland from the summit of Ben Nevis, and trudged the 500-mile Bruce Trail from Niagara to the tip of the Bruce Peninsula. I've driven the highways and back roads of Canada, the USA, and the United Kingdom, and I'm eager to explore them further. I have an extensive bucket list, and I'm well aware that I'm running out of time.*

"*I am, perhaps, a little obsessive and opinionated. Of course I am. I've been accumulating opinions for more than seven decades, but everything I believe is based on the knowledge of others—parents, teachers, colleagues and writers. I'm a fiscal conservative, and I don't believe in magic. Though I don't discount the role of mathematical odds, I believe we create our own futures with every decision we make.*"

Forsyth's published works include *Dafydd* (Fifth Concession Publishing, 2014), a memoir of growing up on an Ontario farm in the 1950s and *Too Cold for Mermaids* (Rock's Mills Press, 2017), which describes his sailing adventures on the Great Lakes, the North Atlantic and the inland waterways of the United States. He continues to write and is currently working on his first novel, which is based on the true story of a war bride who, in 1919, exiled herself from her family and her beloved England for the love of a Canadian soldier.

www.ingramcontent.com/pod-product-compliance
Lightning Source LLC
Chambersburg PA
CBHW030916080526
44589CB00010B/333